A Book of Airplanes

Pushers, Spads, Jennies and Jets

Written and Illustrated by Leonard Everett Fisher

Published by The Dial Press of New York

For My Parents

Man always wanted to fly.

He built wings and flapped them, yet he stayed on the ground. He invented balloons and managed to float on air. He made better wings and silently glided through the sky, but he did not have power to move himself. It was the air that moved him. He needed an airplane!

At last a man in an airplane rose from the ground. He did not go very high, fast, or far. But *he* made the machine move. He was flying!

Any flying machine that is heavier than air, with an engine, wings, and a man to guide it, is an airplane. The first successful flight in an airplane was made by Orville Wright.

Soon other men learned to fly. Many different kinds of airplanes were built. One of these looked like a huge box-kite. Since its large wings were the tail, it always seemed to be flying backwards.

o one dared to fly long distances over water. It was too dangerous. Then, Louis Blériot did. He flew a machine called a monoplane from France to England. People then knew they could fly anywhere in the world.

Most of the first airplanes had propellers connected to the rear of their gasoline engines. They were called Pushers. A Pusher was flown across the United States advertising soda pop. And the trip took almost three months!

Some airplanes began to carry passengers and they were called airliners. One of the first airliners had an outside deck. Passengers were able to take a walk while in flight.

During World War I only military airplanes were built. The Americans used French airplanes called Spads. The Germans had a machine with three wings called a Fokker.

After the war some of the military flyers became flying daredevils. They did amazing tricks in a two-seater training machine called a Jenny.

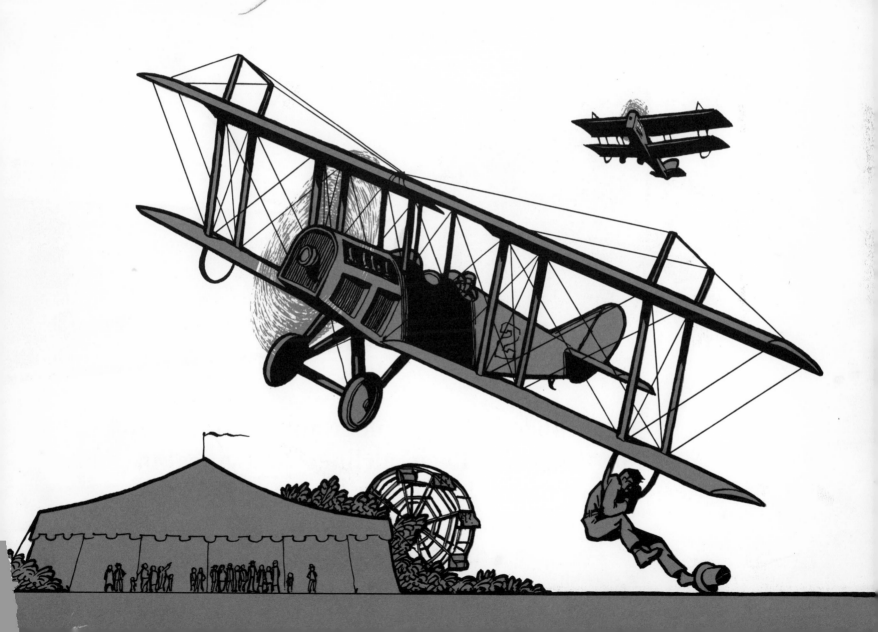

More and more people wanted to travel by air. The Handley Page airliner had a cabin for twelve passengers, but the pilot sat outside!

Bigger and more comfortable airliners were built. The Tin Goose had three engines. Everyone, including the pilot, sat inside.

One of the largest airplanes ever to fly was the Dornier DO-X. It carried almost two hundred people. The DO-X was a flying boat. Twelve engines were needed to give it power.

The Autogiro, invented by Juan de la Cierva, was an unusual airplane. It was able to stay in the air, in one spot, without moving or falling!

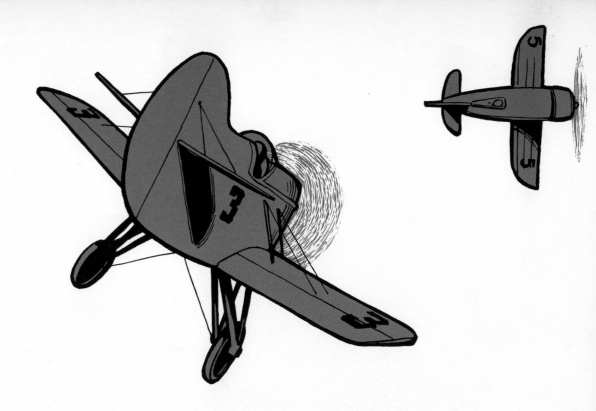

Most people did not want to stand still in the air. They wanted to fly—the faster the better. Big air races were held and tiny airplanes flew with great speed.

The jet engine gave the airplane a new burst of power and speed. Military planes, such as the Shooting Star, streaked like bolts of lightning through the sky.

Man was still not flying as fast as he knew he could. He built a small airplane called the X-1. Finally he flew it faster than sound can travel.

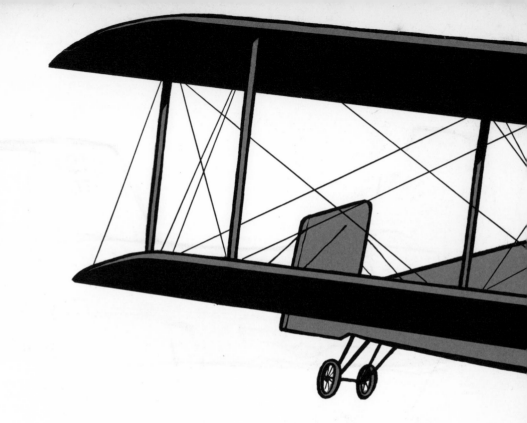

Some day we shall fly to stars and other planets. The machines that will take us through space will be new and different. But we shall always know that powered flight began for man in an airplane!